LORI MCAFEE

THE
REFINERY

A 6-WEEK
BIBLE STUDY
TO AN
ABUNDANT LIFE

Shanty Grove Press

ISBN: 979-8-218-38615-3 (paperback)

To my beloved church family,

This dedication is a small token of my heartfelt gratitude for unwavering support and unconditional love you've shown me. Your prayers have uplifted me, your kindness has healed me, and your faith has inspired me to walk closer with the Lord. May our shared journey be a reflection of God's faithfulness and grace as we support each other and follow His command in Matthew 28.

In hope and love,

Lori

TABLE OF CONTENTS

INTRODUCTION...8-13

1. RECOGNIZE THE VINE WITH RENEWED FAITH.................................14-20
    Introduction...15
    Key Verse..16
    John 15:1-3..17
    The Bible Speaks...18
    Thought-Provoking Questions..19
    Closing Prayer...20

2. EMBRACE THE PRUNING AND THE PURPOSE..................................22-32
    Introduction..23-24
    Key Verse..25
    Isaiah 38:15-19..26
    The Bible Speaks 27
    Lori's Reflections...28
    Thought-Provoking Questions...29-31
    Closing Prayer...32

3. FRUITFULNESS THROUGH ABIDING...34-42
    Introduction..35-36
    Key Verse..36
    Psalm 1:1-3..37
    The Bible Speaks...38
    Lori's Reflections...39
    Thought-Provoking Questions..40
    Closing Prayer...41

4. INTIMATELY INTENTIONAL LIVING..42-52
    Introduction..43-44
    Key Verse..44
    1 Peter 2:9..45
    The Bible Speaks...46
    Lori's Reflections...47
    Thought-Provoking Questions..48
    Closing Prayer...49

TABLE OF CONTENTS

5. NOW REMAIN IN..50-59

    Introduction..51-52

    Key Verse..52

    Philippians 4:13 (ESV)...53

    The Bible Speaks..54-55

    Lori's Reflections...56

    Thought-Provoking Questions...............................57

    Closing Prayer..58

6. ENGAGE IN JOYFUL OBEDIENCE (JOHN 15:14-17)............................60-70

    Introduction..61-62

    Key Verse..63

    Romans 12:1-2 (ESV)..64

    The Bible Speaks..65

    Lori's Reflections...66

    Thought-Provoking Questions...............................67-69

    Closing Prayer..70

CONCLUSION 72-81

    On Prayer 73-76

    Overview of R.E.F.I.N.E. 76-78

    Application of R.E.F.I.N.E. 78-79

    The Vine 81

ABOUT THE AUTHOR..83

"*The vine, our refinery of transformation, shapes our souls through His pruning and purifies our spirits in His embrace. Abiding in the vine, we reap the abundance of promised grace, where faith is refined and love, our yield.*"

INTRODUCTION

Growing up, my parents always planted a garden. Our garden spot was a patch of land that appeared to be created for a time such as this, providing rich soil for sowing and harvesting. The spot was relatively flat, a vast and opened rectangle allowing the sunlight to bathe the plants and the rain to quench their thirst. Each row lain was endless and perfectly straight. Over many years, the practice of gardening became systematically synchronized to serve a purpose and offer support. Every row consisted of fertile soil, deep roots, and manicured and tended plants that would boast lush, vibrant greens and other colors, providing a harvest that fulfilled its fullest potential and purpose.

As an adult, the eyes of my heart see the similarities between my childhood gardening experiences and my life today of abiding in the "true vine." In the gospel of John, Chapter 15, we are given one of the most profound gardening metaphors in the Bible of the vinedresser, the vine, the branches, and the fruit. This metaphor is tucked between Jesus' discussion with His disciples about the anticipation of His death and the promised gift of the Holy Spirit. In Jesus' final farewell, He uses a rich, vibrant, recognizable, and life-sustaining symbol to emphasize the complete and utter dependence and vitality of our constant connection to Him. A life of continual reliance on Christ is essential.

Much different than in my younger days, my garden today is a four-by-eight raised bed. As my sister can vouch, I wasn't much into gardening when I was younger, and that hasn't changed much. So, I only plant a little—just some okra, squash, watermelon, peppers, and maybe a tomato plant or two. No matter the seed or plant or what they may produce, one thing remains the same: when separated from the primary source of nutrients, the branches begin to dry out, and the vegetables or fruit start to shrivel and lose their once-vibrant color. The branches become useless, and the produce rots. And that's what happens to us in life and our walk when we are disconnected from Jesus.

By the end of this study guide, readers will have a deeper understanding of John 15:1-17 and practical ways to apply its teachings. The R.E.F.I.N.E. approach offers a comprehensive framework for personal and spiritual growth, fostering a life of intention, abundance, and transformative love.

John 15:1-17 invites us into a deep, rich understanding of our relationship with Jesus. It calls us to recognize Him as our life source, embrace the growth that comes through life's challenges, remain connected to Him, actively express love, and engage in joyful obedience. By internalizing and living out these teachings, we can bear much fruit and experience the fullness of joy that Jesus promises.

The basis of this study is John 15:5, where Jesus says: "I am the vine; you are the branches. Whoever abides in me and I in him, he it is that bears much fruit, for apart from me you can do nothing." This line perfectly encapsulates the essence of the metaphor represented in John 15, evoking the intimate relationship between Jesus and His followers while underscoring the vital importance of remaining connected to Him. According to John 15, in order for us to gain new life—spiritual vitality, growth, and fruitfulness—the idea of "remaining in" is essential. This conveys the profound truth that apart from Jesus, we cannot bear fruit or fulfill our purpose in life, highlighting the necessity of abiding in Him through faith, obedience, and a love relationship.

There are a few fascinating facts I discovered while researching and preparing for *The Refinery*. The vine and branches metaphor in John 15, discussed earlier, highlights the all-encompassing truth of humanity's dependence on God for sustenance, growth, and purpose—essentially, for our life. The intriguing similarity of the vine, branches, leaves, and fruit extends to all mankind, regardless of an individual's beliefs or background. All people are inherently connected to a power greater than themselves whether they recognize it or not, just as the grapevine branches are interconnected with its vines.

Grapevines, like all plants, have a vascular system which includes veins. These veins are part of the vines' structure, and their essential purpose is to transport water, nutrients, and sugar throughout the plant. This vascular system consists of two main vessels that form a complex network, extending throughout the plant to provide life-giving sustenance. Anyone seeing the similarities yet?

The grapevine has a unique support system that allows it to lean into other plants or structures for support, sustainability, and upward growth. But one detail sealed it for me: most grape leaves are heart-shaped, though this obviously varies depending on the species of grape.

So, let's put all of this together! The vine has a vascular system with two main vessels that serve as conduits for transporting all that's needed to and from the leaves, which is essential for sustaining the life and growth of the grapevine. We, too, have a vascular system that has two main vessels supplying life to our heart.

The way I see it is that even down to the level of our biology, the vine and branches metaphor in John 15 is particularly apt at reinforcing humanity's dependence on Jesus for sustenance, growth, and purpose. Though we may encounter challenges and face discipline, God is constantly refining us to become more fruitful and effective for the kingdom and in our own personal journey with Him. It emphasizes the importance of remaining connected to this source of life, so that we may experience the abundance we have been promised while bearing fruit that contributes to the flourishing of others.

"Just as the roots of a vine intertwine with the earth, drawing sustenance and stability, so must our souls intertwine with Christ, the true vine, drawing from Him our life, our strength, and our purpose."

—Lori McAfee

Have you ever questioned *why* a difficult season crept into your life? Have you ever felt like you were making all the wrong decisions? Do you have habits or impurities that no longer serve you? Do you feel stuck in a rotten cycle of negativity? Do you experience anger, fear, pride, jealousy, selfishness, or envy? Do you struggle with comparison or lack of contentment? Do you feel unseen, unheard, or unloved?

If you do, you are not alone—my answer to such questions is a resounding YES. But it was those difficult seasons that changed me for the better. And that's where *The Refinery* came to life.

The process of self-examination and removing impurities came through a journey I call R.E.F.I.N.E.: Recognize the Vine with Renewed Faith, Embrace the Pruning and Purpose, Fruitfulness through Abiding, Intimately Intentional Living, Now Remain In and Engage in Joyful Obedience (John 15:14-17). The refining process is the fundamental idea in John 15.

Jesus describes himself as the "true vine," God the Father as the "vinedresser," and his followers as the "branches." The true vine cannot exist without the vinedresser, the branches cannot exist without the vine, and the fruit will not bear without the branch abiding in the vine. Fruit-bearing branches are pruned to bear more fruit, and the branches that bear no fruit are taken away.

This metaphor is a powerful lesson about hardship, personal growth, intimacy, and transformation. We often think of pain and challenges as negative experiences, ones that frequently plant seeds of bitterness. However, the teachings in John 15 reframe them as necessary for growth, much like a gardener prunes a vine to increase its yield.

In our personal lives, we'll inevitably face challenges. However, these "prunings" can help us grow stronger, wiser, and more resilient. They strip away unhelpful aspects of our lives and prepare us to bear more fruit in the future. This lesson implores us to view challenges not as roadblocks, but as opportunities for growth.

Finally, John 15 underscores the incredible power and importance of love. Jesus commands his disciples to love one another just as he loved them. Love, in this context, is the fruit that the branches are to bear. In our lives, we, too, can bear this fruit of love. By showing kindness, empathy, and understanding, we make our world a little better.

Importantly, this love isn't just about feelings or emotions. It's about action. It's about making sacrifices for others. The love described in John 15 is radical and transformative, challenging us to love deeply and actively.

In conclusion, the lessons from John 15—renewing faith intimately and intentionally, growth through pruning, and having an abundance of love—provide us with a guide to navigate our lives. They challenge us to recognize and embrace our struggles as opportunities for growth and embody love in our actions. Applying these profound lessons from John 15 in our day-to-day lives can indeed be transformative.

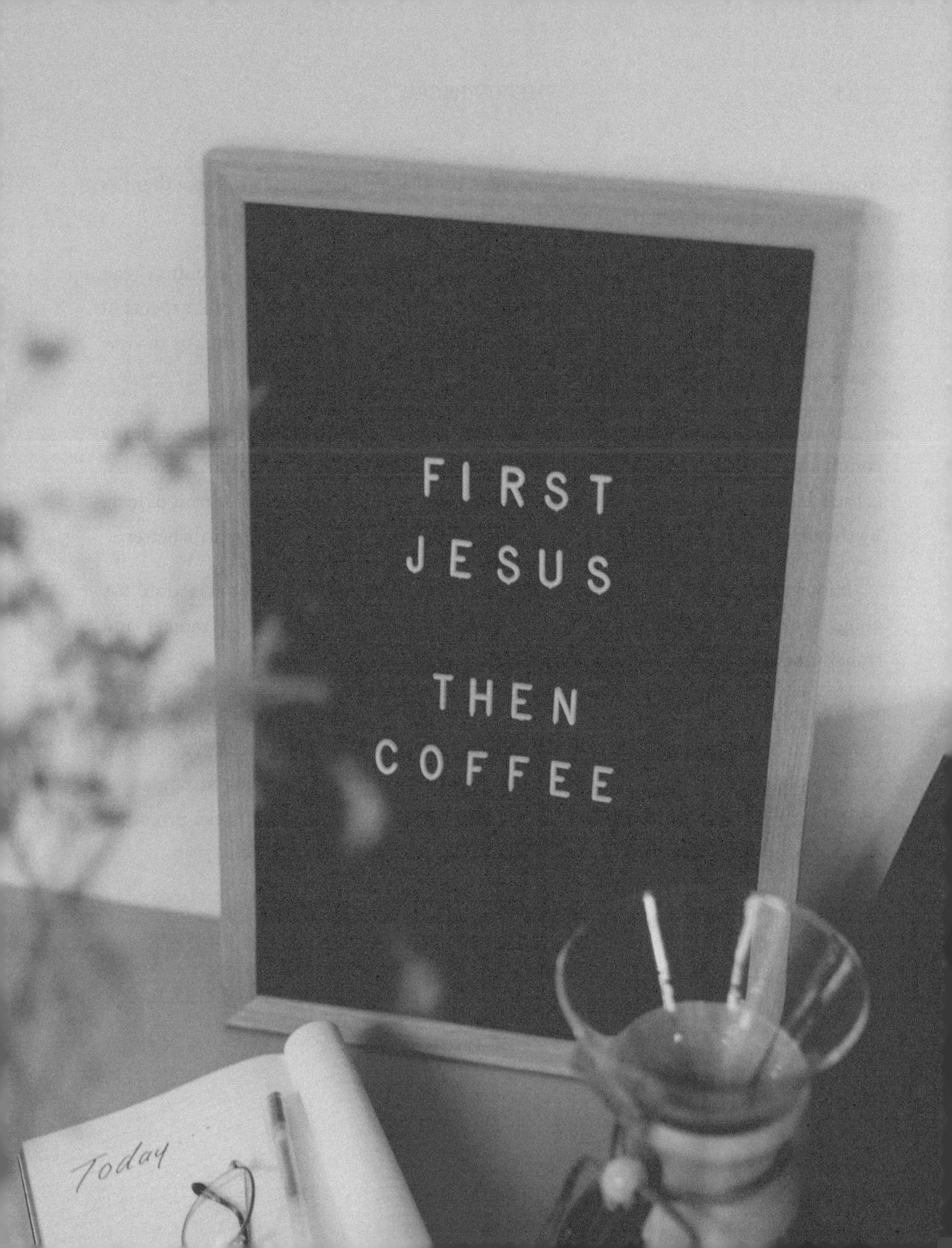
FIRST
JESUS
THEN
COFFEE
Today

1

RECOGNIZE THE VINE WITH RENEWED FAITH

Imagine all your senses are heightened as you gaze through a vineyard. Now, let's take a walk through the lush vibrancy of the hedgerows. Many of us can stand amidst such a sight and miss what's really happening around us. Our faith is often focused on our own gaze rather than the vineyard. In the process, we miss the true vine!

I would sit in and lead Bible studies, attend church every time the doors opened, go to women's retreats, Christian concerts, and mission trips. I did morning devotionals and read God's word—yet something was still missing, and my faith was frail. I knew I was a beloved child of God, but what was it? Once, I sat in San Jose airport for 10 hours after a mission trip and had many conversations about this topic, but I brought only one back to Georgia with me. One of the team leaders and I sat while talking, and she said, "You know, sometimes we have what we are looking for." That was it; I was looking for something miraculous to fill me, and the whole time He was there. The Holy Spirit of Jesus is living inside me. As life intensified, I allowed my faith to be awakened, remembering my identity was in Christ. This conversation reminded me I was already clean and tethered to the vine; I just needed lifting. That day, over 3,000 miles from home, I recognized the true vine with renewed faith and my utter daily dependence on Jesus. Doing things apart from Him would produce nothing of eternal value, a thought that awakened my senses to gaze upon the vine with fresh eyes.

In this section, we'll dive into renewing our faith with a more profound sense of who Jesus is and how to live tethered to the true vine. We will explore the significance of Jesus as the true vine in our lives and the center of our faith. Recognizing the vine with renewed faith draws us to deepen our spiritual roots—living in continual connection and dependence as we deepen our faith and live with Jesus, the true vine. We cultivate our relationship with Him and others, and we shape our thoughts, behaviors, perspectives, and decisions following His instructions, in accordance with our calling and mission.

This is not your typical stroll through familiar Bible passages but an invitation to experience and genuinely recognize the vine with a faith that is fresh, vibrant, and alive. We do this as we grasp what it means to have an intimate bond—a love relationship, if you will—with the life-giving source of our nourishment, grace, and spiritual sustenance.

Key Verse

"I am the true vine and my Father is the vinedresser."

—John 15:1

This verse is the bedrock upon which we build our understanding. To recognize the vine is to acknowledge Christ as the source of our life and strength. But what does it mean to do this with renewed faith?

John 15:1-3

"I am the true vine, and my Father is the vinedresser. Every branch in me that does not bear fruit He takes away, and every branch that does bear fruit He prunes, that it may bear more fruit. Already you are clean because of the word that I have spoken to you."

———

Spend some time and allow the Holy Spirit to speak to you as you recognize the true vine with renewed faith. Jesus declares Himself to be the true vine and God the Father as the vinedresser. It is crucial to recognize Jesus as our source of life and nourishment; apart from Him, we can do nothing. As believers, our identity is to be rooted solely in Christ.

The Bible is rich with references to renewed and deeper faith:

"You will seek me and find me, when you seek me with all your heart."

—Jeremiah 29:13

"Ask, and it will be given to you; seek, and you will find; knock, and it will be opened to you. For everyone who asks receives, and the one who seeks finds, and to the one who knocks it will be opened."

—Matthew 7:7-8

"To put off your old self, which belongs to your former manner of life and is corrupt through deceitful desires, and to be renewed in the spirit of your minds, and to put on the new self, created after the likeness of God in true righteousness and holiness."

—Ephesians 4:22-24

"Create in me a clean heart, O God, and renew a right spirit within me."

—Psalm 51:10

"Now faith is the assurance of things hoped for, the conviction of things not seen."

—Hebrews 11:1

Thought-Provoking Questions

1) Jesus said, "I am the true vine." What does this mean to you?

_____

_____

_____

_____

_____

_____

_____

_____

_____

2) In what ways does your daily life reflect the fruitfulness of being firmly rooted to the true vine, and how might you tend to your spiritual branches to yield more of an abundant harvest reaching your fullest potential and purpose?

_____

_____

_____

_____

_____

_____

_____

_____

_____

Closing Prayer

Oh Father, in this season of renewal, deepen our connection with the true vine, Jesus, the one who is our unfailing source of life and strength. We ask for a revival that roots us deeper in Your love and truth. Through fresh eyes and cleansing of the heart, may we never cease to live in continual connection and dependence on You. Now, ground our soul in the life-giving source of Your grace and love. In the precious holy name of Jesus, we pray.

2

EMBRACE THE PRUNING AND PURPOSE

In the garden of faith, the divine gardener is at work. We are the branches, reaching for the sun, rooted in the true vine. But growth is not without its moments of cutting back, of strategic losses for more significant gains. This chapter is an invitation to understand the transformative process of spiritual pruning, where every snip of the divine gardener's shears is purposeful, leading us to a fuller, more fruitful existence.

Jesus speaks of branches being pruned to be more fruitful. This symbolizes our trials and tribulations, which ultimately refine and help us grow. Pruning is vital for growth, and in this chapter, we'll explore how life's challenges can be opportunities for personal transformation.

When faced with difficulties, we can ask God what He wants us to learn from them rather than why they happen to us. Adversity, at some point, will impact our lives, and it does not discriminate. As humans, we will receive the deep cuts of difficult seasons that will leave scars—invisible, but scars nonetheless.

One day, as I was talking with my sister, we talked about how a difficult season of our lives changed us for the better. We allowed God to remove any impurities. Regardless of what they resulted from, they were holding us back from living our created purpose, and the branches that were not producing fruit needed to be pruned away. That day, we both agreed with gratitude that if we did not go through this pruning process, our lives would not become as they are today: abundantly fruitful, resiliently peaceful, and genuinely content.

In my years of life experience, I have discovered that it isn't just the pruning itself, but our response to it. Our surrendered obedience to the pruning is often where we meet the person we were created to be. My sister and I could have looked at various trials, challenges, heartaches, obstacles, valleys, and difficult seasons as reasons to harden our hearts, close our fists, and water the seeds of bitterness. But here's the responsive part: doing those things instead of embracing the pruning and purpose would have left us no room to cultivate and tend to the fruits of joy, hope, peace, or love.

Trials, challenges, detours, and difficulties can often make us feel as though God is far from us, but in these times, God is still very present. In the pruning process, painful but necessary for our purpose, we can stand firm in our faith knowing God remains in us when we remain in Him.

Key Verse

"Every branch in me that does not bear fruit He takes away, and every branch that does bear fruit He prunes, that it may bear more fruit."

—John 15:2

This scripture is a cornerstone of our exploration of Embrace the Pruning and Purpose. Embracing the pruning means gratefully welcoming wise and loving discipline, understanding that it shapes us to bear more fruit, while embracing the purpose is to hold fast to the promise that God is at work within and around us, using all things to work for the good. What does the pruning process look like in the context of embracing it for purpose?

Isaiah 5:5-7

"And now I will tell you what I will do to my vineyard. I will remove its hedge, and it shall be devoured; I will break down its wall, and it shall be trampled down. I will make it a waste; it shall not be pruned or hoed, and briers and thorns shall grow up; I will also command the clouds that they rain no rain upon it. For the vineyard of the Lord of hosts is the house of Israel, and the men of Judah are His pleasant planting."

How have you or do you see God's hand in the pruning process of your life, and what has it done for you? If the process has caused the seed of bitterness to sprout, pray for God's strength to relinquish control and surrender to His pruning for your deliverance. If the process has helped you grow closer to Him, now is the time to reflect on what God has or is doing.

To embrace the true vine and open our hearts to the pruning process is a call to repentance and prayer, that we may seek the sustainer of life and trust in the purpose behind the pruning: the removal of what no longer serves us so that we may produce much fruit.

The Bible is rich with references to pruning and growth:

"For before the harvest, when the blossom is over, and the flower becomes a ripening grape, He cuts off the shoots with pruning hooks, and, spreading branches, He lops off and clears away."

—Isaiah 18:5

"Every tree that does not bear good fruit is cut down and thrown into the fire."

—Matthew 7:19

"And He told this parable: 'A man had a fig tree planted in his vineyard, and he came seeking fruit on it and found none. And he said to the vinedresser, 'Look, for three years now I have come seeking fruit on this fig tree, and I find none. Cut it down. Why should it use up the ground?' And he answered him, 'Sir, let it alone this year also, until I dig around it and put on manure. Then if it should bear fruit next year, well and good; but if not, you can cut it down.'"

—Luke 13:6-9

"For the moment all discipline seems painful rather than pleasant, but later it yields the peaceful fruit of righteousness to those who have been trained by it."

—Hebrews 12:11

Lori's Reflections

"In the divine economy of growth, loss is not a deficit but an investment in a more abundant harvest."

"The shears of divine pruning are guided by hands that know the architecture of our souls better than we do."

"Through the lens of renewed faith, the cuts of pruning are seen not as losses but as preparations for new growth."

Thought-Provoking Questions

1) As a believer, the fruit in our life should be a reflection of the true vine; this is our integrity, character, actions, attitude, and behavior. Where in your life is the reflection visible of Jesus? What needs pruning?

_____

_____

_____

_____

_____

_____

2) Can you recall a time when you felt like you were being pruned? What did you learn from that experience?

_____

_____

_____

_____

_____

3) How can you approach future challenges with the mindset of embracing the pruning and purpose?

_____

_____

_____

_____

_____

Thought-Provoking Questions

4) Reflect on a time when you experienced pruning in your life. What was removed, and what richer fruits did it allow you to bear?

_____
_____
_____
_____
_____
_____
_____
_____
_____
_____

5) Can you identify areas in your spiritual practice that might need the loving discipline of pruning?

_____
_____
_____
_____
_____
_____
_____
_____
_____
_____

Thought-Provoking Questions

6) How does your understanding of purpose shift when you view your challenges as the vinedresser's pruning?

_____

_____

_____

_____

_____

_____

_____

_____

_____

_____

_____

7) Assess your life's branches. Which bear fruit? Which are barren? Contemplate where pruning might encourage new growth.

_____

_____

_____

_____

_____

_____

_____

_____

_____

_____

_____

Closing Prayer

Oh Father, the vinedresser, with hands that spoke the world into existence, we submit to Your loving care. As You prune us, help us to see beyond the immediate pain to the greater purpose You have for us. Teach us to embrace the cutting away of what is no longer needed, so that we may grow more deeply in love with the true vine, our source of life and strength. Grant us the courage to let go, the discernment to assess, the faith to move forward, and the wisdom to bear fruit that nourishes and sustains. In the precious name of Jesus, we pray. Amen.

3

FRUITFULNESS THROUGH ABIDING

"A believer may pass through much affliction, and yet secure very little blessing from it all. Abiding in Christ is the secret of securing all that the Father meant the discipline to bring us."
—*Andrew Murray*

Don't we all want to live a fruitful life? Several years ago, a couple began coming to our church. I heard their miracle story and I knew God was the only answer behind it—and as time passed and I become more acquainted with the couple, I saw the power of abiding more and more. The husband's body had been 70 percent burned from a meth explosion, and he was given a *zero* percent chance to live—but he survived. Though she was an addict as well, his wife was faithful and dedicated; her parents were devoted abiders of the word of God and the power of prayer, and for many years, they prayed for their daughter and her husband.

As the wife sat outside the hospital on a park bench one day, the Holy Spirit began to stir in her soul. She recalled the day she accepted the Lord Jesus Christ as her savior and her parents' countless prayers at the same time God was working on her husband, a scorched soul in need of heart surgery. Fast forward 15 years, and he is serving as our Associate Pastor and overseer of Celebrate Recovery, teaching in drug court and many other things I'm sure I'm not aware of. Meanwhile, his wife is leading women inside and outside the church while serving as a pastor's wife.

The lives of this couple are the fruitfulness through abiding that began from their parents' abiding in God's word and their faithfulness in prayer. Not only did the lives of this couple transform, but they are also touching countless other lives daily as a result.

The richness of an abundant life comes in fruitfulness through abiding and allows us to saturate in the fertile soil of God's word—where sanctification, cleansing, and transformation toward His goodness are cultivated. Abiding in Jesus, and staying connected to the true vine, is key to bearing fruit in our lives. Apart from Him, we can do nothing.

In this section, we'll discuss the concept of abiding in Christ and how it leads to fruitfulness: living with a steadfast, persistent faith, exploring the power of a life deeply rooted in the spiritual practices of reading and meditating on God's word, faithful and steadfast in prayer, and living in daily unity with the true vine.

Key Verse

"Abide in me, and I in you. As the branch cannot bear fruit by itself unless it abides in the vine, neither can you unless you abide in me."

—John 15:4

This verse calls us to a life with Christ that remains connected, deeply rooted, frequently fostered, and routinely rested. To abide is to live in continuous, unbroken fellowship with the true vine. But what does this intimate relationship entail for a believer seeking fruitfulness?

Abiding is an active, living, breathing commitment. It means to dwell in His word, His love, and His way. Fruitfulness emerges from this deep, sustained connection—a visible representation that flows through our veins.

Psalm 1:1-3

"Blessed is the man who walks not in the counsel of the wicked, nor stands in the way of sinners, nor sits in the seat of scoffers; but his delight is in the law of the Lord, and on his law he meditates day and night. He is like a tree planted by streams of water that yields its fruit in its season, and its leaf does not wither. In all that he does, he prospers."

Are your roots deeply planted in the streams of God's word, drawing sustenance and strength from your relationship with Him? How might you deepen your connection to experience greater spiritual growth and fulfillment?

The Bible offers rewarding insights into a fruitful life:

"But the fruit of the Spirit is love, joy, peace, patience, kindness, goodness, faithfulness, gentleness, self-control; against such things there is no law. And those who belong to Christ Jesus have crucified the flesh with its passions and desires. If we live by the Spirit, let us also keep in step with the Spirit."

—Galatians 5:22-25

"And it is my prayer that your love may abound more and more, with knowledge and all discernment, so that you may approve what is excellent, and so be pure and blameless for the day of Christ, filled with the fruit of righteousness that comes through Jesus Christ, to the glory and praise of God."

—Philippians 1:9-11

"So as to walk in a manner worthy of the Lord, fully pleasing to him: bearing fruit in every good work and increasing in the knowledge of God."

—Colossians 1:10

"But the wisdom from above is first pure, then peaceable, gentle, open to reason, full of mercy and good fruits, impartial, and sincere. And a harvest of righteousness is sown in peace by those who make peace."

—James 3:17-18

Lori's Reflections

"To abide in the true vine is to find the rhythm of grace that orchestrates the symphony of fruitfulness in our lives."

"Fruitfulness is the silent witness of our abode in Him; a life lived in the shelter of the Almighty cannot help but flourish."

"Abiding is the art of remaining steadfast under the Master's hand, cultivating the beauty that comes from divine intimacy."

Thought-Provoking Questions

1) What practices help you to abide in the true vine, and how have they changed the fruits you bear?

_____

_____

_____

_____

_____

_____

_____

2) In what ways do you struggle to maintain a daily dwelling in the presence of God?

_____

_____

_____

_____

_____

_____

3) How can you cultivate a deeper sense of abiding in your life, and what might be the first fruits of this commitment?

_____

_____

_____

_____

_____

_____

Closing Prayer

Dear Lord, in the quite pureness of Your presence, we seek to abide. May we remain securely fastened to the true vine, drawing life from Your endless reservoirs of nourishment in rest and love. Let our fruit be plentiful, our faith deep-rooted, and our spirits intertwined with Yours. Infuse our every moment with the essence of Your being, that we may truly live, move, and have our being solely rooted in You. Cultivate in us a harvest that brings joy to Your heart and blessing to the world. Through the nurturing presence of Jesus, our true vine, we pray. Amen.

4

INTIMATELY INTENTIONAL LIVING

Living a life marked by intentional intimacy is a foundational principle to the Christian life. This principle is brought to life when a Christian is united with Jesus and the two navigate life as one cohesive entity. We are given purpose and direction through God's version of intentionality for our lives. We don't have to strive but simply follow Him, and live according to His will. The central beauty of this relationship mirrors the symbolic connection between the vine and its fruit-bearing branches—a union rooted in intimacy and cultivated growth.

My own understanding of what it means to have an intimate relationship with God was shaped by my relationship with my husband. To truly align my life with God's will, I realized how vital it was that I know Him deeply. This meant intentionally investing time to become familiar with the presence of God in a very practical and constant way, much like the effort I put into getting to know my husband when we first met. It took me years to recognize my need for an intimate and intentional life with God. This led me to ponder: How might my relationship with my husband have been if my love relationship with God had been an intentional part of my life from the start?

Since falling deeply in love with God, I can recall numerous situations, events, and challenges throughout my life where my intimate relationship with Him became my strength, the very breath in my lungs. This deeply tender closeness I now cherish with God—and that you can experience, too—grew because of God's grace in revealing Himself to us. Jesus calls us into a relationship of mutual abiding, a deep, intimate connection that we may be pruned for a life of purpose through intentional living. As I continue my journey with Christ, I've learned that an intimate and intentional life with Him enriches all of my other relationships, making them much sweeter.

As your intimate love relationship with Christ deepens and you seek life with intentionality while viewing your experiences through the lens of the branch, you begin to see God in every aspect of your life. This section invites us into the realm of intimately intentional living, encouraging us to align our daily actions, choices, and decisions with the purposeful heartbeat of the true vine. In doing so, we not only grow closer to God, but we also learn to live in a way that reflects His love and purpose in every relationship and circumstance.

Key Verse

"You do not choose me, but I chose you and appointed you that you should go and bear fruit and that your fruit should abide, so that whatever you ask the Father in my name, he may give it to you. These things I command you, so that you will love one another."

—John 15:16-17

To live a life that is intimately intentional is to live a life with boundless assurance in God that our days are saturated with joy and expectancy. Intimately intentional living calls us to delicately engage with life's details. Our actions become offerings, our decisions become declarations of faith, and our life becomes a living testament to the love and grace of the true vine.

1 Peter 2:9

"But you are a chosen race, a royal priesthood, a holy nation, a people for His own possession, that you may proclaim the excellencies of Him who called you out of darkness into His marvelous light."

As a branch of the true vine, we are reminded of our identity and purpose as followers of Christ in this verse. We are God's most prized possession, a chosen race, a royal priesthood, and a holy nation. It is for His glory that we proclaim the excellencies of who called us out of darkness into the light of His love. It's through understanding and living out the purpose of our lives as His branches, which bear fruit in every aspect of our lives, all while loving deeply as a reflection of the character and love of Christ to the world around us.

How does the realization that you have been specifically chosen by God to proclaim His excellencies and bear lasting fruit shape the way you live your daily life? Are there areas in your life where you feel called to step out more boldly in faith, reflecting His light and love?

The Bible speaks to us about a life of intentionality and intimacy:

"Whatever you do, work heartily, as for the Lord and not for men."

—Colossians 3:23

"Look carefully then how you walk, not as unwise but as wise, making the best use of the time, because the days are evil."

—Ephesians 5:15-16

"So, whether you eat or drink, or whatever you do, do all to the glory of God."

—1 Corinthians 10:31

"But be doers of the word, and not hearers only, deceiving yourselves."

—James 1:22

"In the same way, let your light shine before others, so that they may see your good works and give glory to your Father who is in heaven."

—Matthew 5:16

Lori's Reflections

"Intimately intentional living is a thread woven each day of our lives, weaving us into a masterpiece of purpose."

"When we align our will with God, every act becomes an act of worship, every choice a chorus of praise."

"Living with intention is the vibrant color painting our lives with strokes of faithfulness, hope, and love—the colors of the Spirit."

Thought-Provoking Questions

1) What does it mean for you to live intentionally in your everyday life, and how does this reflect your intimacy with God?

_____

_____

_____

_____

_____

_____

2) Can you identify moments when your routine actions diverged from your spiritual intentions? How can you realign them?

_____

_____

_____

_____

_____

_____

3) What steps can you take today to ensure your actions are deliberate expressions of your faith?

_____

_____

_____

_____

_____

Closing Prayer

Lord of all infinite wisdom, you orchestrate the universe with intentional grace. Guide us in the tenderness of intimately intentional living. May our lives be like tuned instruments, each note played in harmony with where you are working daily. In every decision, in every action, let our hearts become us one with Yours, creating a symphony of intentionality and faith that resonates with Your will. Help us to remember that in the ordinariness of life, we are privileged to the extraordinariness of Your love and grace. Through the strength and guidance of Jesus, the true vine, we commit to living intentionally, with hearts that crave your presence. Amen.

5

NOW REMAIN IN

In the holiness of our spiritual journey, to "now remain in" is to hold steadfast, to anchor ourselves in the enduring truth of our identity being rooted in Christ and our endless love relationship with God. This chapter is paramount in the constancy of abiding. It's an invitation to understand, embody, and rest in the call to be unwavering branches of the true vine—a life of continual, intentional reliance on Jesus. When we remain in, He remains in.

Okay, I have a confession: this one was challenging for me. The "N" in R.E.F.I.N.E. has changed numerous times. There is no doubt in my mind that God was pruning and refining me to before I could grasp what He had for this section.

I love to slalom ski. I am very much an amateur, but nevertheless, I truly enjoy the thrill of power, speed, balance, and ability that encompasses a good ride. When I was a teenager, my dad taught us how to ski. I will never forget him surprising us with a bright green and blue O'Brien slalom ski as we were heading out to the lake for an enjoyable family afternoon. I sat on the back of the boat, positioned my left foot in the front boot and my right foot directly behind, and then slid off onto the water, holding onto the rope for dear life. My dad began giving me very direct guidance on how to make my first experience amazing. I specifically remember his words: "I'm going to have to tug you a bit! Now, you remain directly behind the boat. Allow the power of the boat to pull you out of the water. If you will stay in the smooth water, you will have the ride of your life." Now, almost 40 years later, I still follow his guidance: the promise of an incredible ride if *I now remain.*

Just as my dad gave me specific instructions on how to love the sport of skiing, Jesus gives us specific instructions on how to have a fruitful, abundant life and to remain. The fruitfulness that Jesus promises by remaining in Him is more than just potential; it's the certainty and assurance of a fruitful life.

Key Verse

"Abide in me, and I in you. As the branch cannot bear fruit by itself unless it abides in the vine, neither can you, unless you abide in me."

—John 15:4

To "now remain" is to live in the perpetual presence of the true vine, to maintain an unbroken communion with Christ, and to let His lifeblood flow through our veins without hindrance despite what may occur around us.

"Now remain" signals us to a place beyond the initial connection to the vine, into a realm of continuous, conscious presence in Him. It's a call to enduring faithfulness, to a persistent state of spiritual flourishing that comes from an unyielding union with Jesus.

Philippians 4:13

"I can do all things through Him who strengthens me."

Our power is not of our own strength or capability but in remaining and abiding in Christ. As we remain in a relationship with Jesus, the sustainer of life, this connection is the source of our spiritual vitality and fruitfulness. In order for us to navigate life's challenges and fulfill our God-given potential, we must remain rooted in Christ and draw our resilience from His strength within us.

In what areas of your life are you trying to bear fruit on your own strength? How might your efforts and outcomes change if you were to grasp the truth that your ability to thrive and succeed comes through remaining and abiding in Christ and relying on His strength?

The Bible speaks to us on God's love as we remain tethered to him:

"Abide in me, and I in you. As the branch cannot bear fruit by itself, unless it abides in the vine, neither can you, unless you abide in me. I am the vine; you are the branches. Whoever abides in me and I in him, he it is that bears much fruit, for apart from me you can do nothing. If anyone does not abide in me, he is thrown away like a branch and withers; and the branches are gathered, thrown into the fire, and burned. If you abide in me, and my words abide in you, ask whatever you wish, and it will be done for you. By this my Father is glorified, that you bear much fruit and so prove to be my disciples. As the Father has loved me, so have I loved you. Abide in my love. If you keep my commandments, you will abide in my love, just as I have kept my Father's commandments and abide in his love."

—John 15:4-10

"But I am like a green olive tree in the house of God. I trust in the steadfast love of God forever and ever. I will thank You forever, because You have done it. I will wait for Your name, for it is good, in the presence of the godly."

—Psalm 52:8-9

"Let what you heard from the beginning abide in you. If what you heard from the beginning abides in you, then you too will abide in the Son and in the Father."

—*1 John 2:24*

"But you, beloved, building yourselves up in your most holy faith and praying in the Holy Spirit, keep yourselves in the love of God, waiting for the mercy of our Lord Jesus Christ that leads to eternal life."

—*Jude 1:20-21*

Lori's Reflections

"To 'now remain' is to live with the true vine as our eternal compass, orienting every thought, every action, every moment to His divine purpose."

"The steadfast branch knows that its strength is not in the firmness of its grip on the vine, but in the vitality of life in the vinedresser's hands."

"Remaining is not a passive state—it is the active pursuit of constancy in Christ, a daily decision to dwell in His presence."

Thought-Provoking Questions

1) What does it mean for you to "now remain" in your spiritual walk, and how does this manifest in your daily life?

_____

_____

_____

_____

_____

2) Can you identify moments when you've struggled to remain in Him? What helped you to reconnect?

_____

_____

_____

_____

_____

3) How can the practice of "remaining" change your perspective on trials and tribulations?

_____

_____

_____

_____

_____

Closing Prayer

Heavenly Father, in Your unending faithfulness, guide us to steadfastly "now remain" in Your Son. As we cling to the true vine, nurture within us a harvest rich with love, joy, peace, and all the fruits of Your Spirit. May our enduring presence in You reveal the profound depths of Your grace, and in this divine constancy, let our lives reflect the radiance of Your glory. Through Jesus Christ, our sustaining true vine, we pray for the courage and grace to now remain in You, always. Amen.

6

ENGAGE IN JOYFUL OBEDIENCE

(1 JOHN 5:3)

Obedience to God's commands is a source of profound joy. Jesus calls us not only to obedience but to joyful obedience, rooted in love and leading to complete joy. As we engage in joyful obedience, we enter into a life of deep reverence and glorious liberation. A life of mere compliance misses the richness of experiencing the fullness of joyful obedience.

The Costa Rican jungle can be as threatening as it is thrilling. Several years ago while on a mission trip, we were into the depths of the wild only to arrive at the most breathtaking sight: a waterfall standing confidently as its beauty led the dancing rainbows circling us. Everyone was accounted for except my friend and her son. When I asked where they were, my friend assured me that my friend's precious son wouldn't leave his mom's side. The path that led us to this amazing waterfall was about a half mile long, laden with large, slick rocks to cross, monkeys screaming at us from the treetops, and who knows what kinds of other kill-you-instantly creatures that were silently waiting to strike.

I knew my friend was with her son back at the van and thought of all the fun he was missing when God immediately prompted me to take the son's place. Just for the record, I'm scared of my own shadow, so this prompting, not gonna lie, came with a bit of resistance. But I knew that God was giving me instructions to sit with my friend while her son enjoyed the jungle experience. He wouldn't allow any of my "fears" to swallow me whole. As I made the trek back and had my eyes set on my friend, I yelled for her son to take off and enjoy himself; I had already seen the glorious sights, and now it was his turn. For the rest of the afternoon, a deeper friendship than I could've ever imagined started growing, lush as the jungle, and that friendship is still as strong today.

Out of my love for her and our abiding obedience to God, our friendship is a testament to engaging in joyful obedience—an abiding joy that warms the soul, full of life and colors as vibrant as the Costa Rican jungle. We can seek to obey God's commands joyfully, understanding that His commandments are rooted in love. This could involve reframing obedience not as a burden but as an expression of our love for God. Actually, a surrendered obedience is freeing, leading to a fuller, more joyful life.

In the unfolding story of our faith, obedience is not a burden to be borne with resignation but a melody to be sung with joy. This chapter explores the harmonious act of engaging in joyful obedience, a dance with the divine choreographed by love and a willingness to follow His lead.

Key Verse

"If you keep my commandments, you will abide in my love, just as I have kept my Father's commandments and abide in his love. These things I have spoken to you, that my joy may be in you, and that your joy may be full."

—John 15:10-11

Joyful obedience is the act of embracing God's commandments with a heart full of joy. It is a sign of our trust in Him, a testament to our belief that His way is not only right but the path to true happiness. Engaging in joyful obedience involves understanding that our obedience is a response to the love we receive from Christ, the true vine, and our love for Him. It is not about reluctant compliance but embracing His will with a spirit of joy.

Romans 12:1-2

"I appeal to you therefore, brothers, by the mercies of God, to present your bodies as a living sacrifice, holy and acceptable to God, which is your spiritual worship. Do not be conformed to this world, but be transformed by the renewal of your mind, that by testing you may discern what is the will of God, what is good and acceptable and perfect."

———

When we fully offer ourselves to God as an act of worship, we feel the urge within ourselves to resist the patterns of the world and embrace transformation through the renewal of our minds. This transformation allows us to understand, engage with, and live out God's will, which is described as good, pleasing, and perfect. This passage underlines the idea that true obedience to God is a joyful act of surrender, one that leads to deeper understanding and joyous fulfillment where we experience Him and His purpose for our lives.

The Bible speaks to us about joyful obedience:

"For I find my delight in Your commandments, which I love. I will lift up my hands toward Your commandments, which I love, and I will meditate on Your statutes."

—Psalm 119:47-48

"For this is the love of God, that we keep His commandments. And His commandments are not burdensome."

—1 John 5:3

"Therefore, my beloved, as you have always obeyed, so now, not only as in my presence but much more in my absence, work out your own salvation with fear and trembling, for it is God who works in you, both to will and to work for His good pleasure."

—Philippians 2:12-13

"Each one must give as he has decided in his heart, not reluctantly or under compulsion, for God loves a cheerful giver."

—2 Corinthians 9:7

"Because you did not serve the Lord your God with joyfulness and gladness of heart, for the abundance of everything, therefore you shall serve your enemies whom the Lord will send against you, in hunger and thirst, in nakedness, and lacking everything. And He will put a yoke of iron on your neck until He has destroyed you."

—Deuteronomy 28:47-48

Lori's Reflections

"Obedience without joy is like a symphony without melody—technically sound but missing the heart of music."

"The joy of the Lord is our strength, and in the strength of that joy, our obedience finds its rhythm."

"In the hands of God, our acts of obedience become brush strokes in the masterpiece of His purpose."

Thought-Provoking Questions

1) How does understanding obedience as an expression of love change your willingness to obey?

_____

_____

_____

_____

_____

_____

2) What does joyful obedience look like in your daily life, and in what areas do you find it challenging to maintain?

_____

_____

_____

_____

_____

_____

3) How can you cultivate a heart that finds joy in following God's commandments?

_____

_____

_____

_____

_____

_____

Thought-Provoking Questions

4) Can you recall a time when obedience resulted in unexpected joy?

_____

_____

_____

_____

_____

_____

_____

5) How does presenting your life as a "living sacrifice" change your perspective on obedience to God?

_____

_____

_____

_____

_____

_____

_____

6) In what ways can you seek to renew your mind daily, so that you may discern and joyfully follow God's will for your life?

_____

_____

_____

_____

_____

_____

Thought-Provoking Questions

7) Reflecting on the transformation that comes from God, how can you cultivate a joyful act of surrendered obedience that transcends mere duty or resentful compliance and becomes a heartfelt expression of love for Him?

_____

_____

_____

_____

_____

_____

_____

_____

_____

_____

Closing Prayer

Father of pure joy, from whom every good and perfect gift descends, infuse our hearts with the joy that comes from knowing You. As we walk in obedience to Your word, let it be with a spirit of gladness, singing a hymn of devotion to Your will. May our deeds of faith be acts of worship, our compliance a celebration, and our submission a song of gratitude. Let the joy of Your presence be the fountain from which our obedience flows, so that in keeping Your commands, our joy—and Yours—may be made complete. Through the true vine, Jesus Christ, we pray. Amen.

THE REFINERY

CONCLUSION

R.E.F.I.N.E.! As Jesus said, "I am the true vine." Jesus is the sustainer of life when our identity is solely rooted in the I AM! In the final chapter, we'll discuss integrating the lessons of John 15 into everyday life. We'll provide guidance for the ongoing journey of spiritual growth and how to apply these teachings in various aspects of life, including prayer, personal relationships, and professional settings.

John 15:1-17 invites us into a deep, rich understanding of our relationship with Jesus. It calls us to recognize Him as our life source, embrace the growth that comes through life's challenges, remain connected to Him, actively express love, and engage in joyful obedience. By internalizing and living out these teachings, we can bear much fruit and experience the fullness of joy that Jesus promises.

By the end of this study guide, readers will have a deeper understanding of John 15:1-17 and practical ways to apply its teachings. The R.E.F.I.N.E. approach offers a comprehensive framework for personal and spiritual growth, fostering a life of intention, abundance, and transformative love. Putting that framework into action begins with prayer.

On Prayer

Prayer is a transformative act of intimacy with God involving gratitude, dependency, alignment with His will, and a desire for spiritual growth. By grounding prayers in Scripture, believers deepen their connection with Jesus, inviting His presence, guidance, and sanctifying work into their lives. Our prayer life is essential for bearing fruit in the Christian life; it is of vital importance to remain connected to Jesus, the true vine, in order to produce fruit.

Prayer is being an active participant in a fruitful life, because it is one of the primary forms of communication believers have with Jesus. Through prayer, we maintain an active and intimate relationship with Jesus, seeing His guidance, strength and empowerment to live out our faith. With this in mind, we will quickly explore how prayer relates to the concept of abiding in Jesus and bearing fruit:

Connection With Jesus: Prayer serves as a means of maintaining a close, intimate connection with Jesus. Prayer is not just a one-way communication; ask Jesus and listen. (Matthew 6:6-13, 1 Peter 3:12)

Dependence on God: Prayer reflects believers' dependence on God for everything. (2 Corinthians 12:7-10)

Alignment With God's Will: Through prayer, believers seek for their lives to be in alignment with God's will, surrendering their desires and submitting to His plans. (Proverbs 3:5-6 and Isaiah 55:8-9)

Faithful Confidence in Jesus: Prayer is evidence of having faithful confidence God's word. As Jesus said, "Ask and receive." By abiding in Jesus, we pray with boldness and to experience answered prayers. This also produces transformation and growth in those who walk with Christ. (Matthew 7:7, John 15:7, and 1 John 5:14)

Always remember that prayer is an essential aspect of abiding in Jesus, serving as a means of connection and intimacy, dependency, alignment with God's will, and faithful confidence. By maintaining a vibrant prayer life, we deepen our relationship with Jesus and experience the fullness of life that comes from abiding in Him.

"Abiding in Him infuses our prayers with boldness, aligning our desires with His will. In this intimate connection, our confidence grows and faith flourishes as we witness the undeniable answers to our prayers."

—*Lori McAfee*

With all these lessons in mind, I love to pray God's word back to Him. For inspiration and guidance on how to do this in your own life, here are few examples of how this can look:

"Heavenly Father, I lift my voice in prayer, mindful of the promise that Your eyes are upon the righteous and Your ears attentive to their prayers. Lord, I thank You for Your constant presence and care in my life. Help me to walk in righteousness and integrity before You, knowing that my prayers are heard and answered according to Your perfect will. Grant me the wisdom to discern Your guidance and the courage to follow it. May my life be a testament to Your faithfulness and love. In Jesus' name, amen."

"Lord, I confess my dependency on You for every aspect of my life. I surrender my worries, fears, and anxieties to You, trusting in Your provision and care. Help me to seek Your will above my own, aligning my desires with Your plans and purposes. Guide me in the decisions I make, that they may bring glory to Your name. In your son Jesus' precious, holy name, amen."

"Heavenly Father, I come before You in prayer, grateful for the assurance that if we ask anything according to Your will, You hear us. Lord, as I lift my requests to You, I seek Your

wisdom and discernment to align my prayers with Your perfect will. Help me to surrender my desires and trust in Your plan, knowing that Your ways are higher than mine. Grant me the faith to believe that You will answer according to Your timing and purpose. May Your will be done in my life, and may Your name be glorified through the answers to my prayers. In Jesus' name, amen."

Overview of R.E.F.I.N.E.

With this approach to prayer, you will have a deeper receptivity to God's will and His plan for your life, as well as a better understanding for how to use this framework. To refresh ourselves, here are the principles of R.E.F.I.N.E.:

Recognize the Vine with Renewed Faith: Acknowledge Jesus as the cornerstone of existence. Without this recognition, one may feel lost and without purpose. Embracing Jesus as the true vine means realizing that He is the source of all life and sustenance. This recognition renews our faith and sets the foundation for growth.

Embrace the Pruning and Purpose: Understand that pruning is a divine process designed to strengthen and prepare us for greater things. By embracing these trials as necessary for growth, the solution becomes clear: pruning leads to a more fruitful existence, aligning our lives with God's will.

Fruitfulness Through Abiding: In the everlasting pursuit of a life that overflows with abundance, we find abiding. A life of fruitfulness comes from dwelling deeply in the presence of Christ. When one is rooted in the truth of God's word and remains tethered to the true vine, we see His faithfulness produce fruitfulness that fulfills a lasting purpose.

Intimately Intentional Living: Replace mere existence with intimate, intentional living aligned with Christ's teachings. Our life is secure through our daily cadence of stepping in harmony with the rhythm of the true vine and being deeply rooted in a love relationship. Through the lens of Jesus, every moment becomes an open door to bodily proclaim the purposeful rhythm that illustrates a life of divine intention.

Now Remain In: A call to deeply root ourselves in the unshakable truth of our identity in Christ and our eternal bond of love with God throughout faith's journey. This is a journey that is in the realm of constant, mindful presence of the vine, a life of deliberate and continued reliance of abiding in Him and Him in us. It's an invitation to enduring faithfulness, a purposeful state of spiritual growth that flourishes in steadfast union with Jesus.

Engage in Joyful Obedience: Embrace the joy that comes from obedience to God's will. Disobedience leads to a disconnected and unfulfilled life, but joyous obedience aligns us within God's plan. A life of surrendered obedience is both freeing and fulfills the very essence of the freedom Christ offers: a freedom that flourishes in a life of resounding joy.

Application of R.E.F.I.N.E.

With this in mind, it's important to remind yourself to fully embody this framework in your usual responsibilities and relationships, and to remember to allow God's love and grace to work through you and with you in the process. To that end, here are some important ways to apply these principles in your day-to-day life:

Recognize the Vine with Renewed Faith: Each morning, begin with acknowledging Jesus as the source of your life. Pray for insight to see His hand at work, and for faith that is alive and active.

Embrace the Pruning and Purpose: When you encounter trials or disciplines, welcome them as opportunities for growth. Reflect on what God may be pruning from your life and how this is preparing you for future fruitfulness.

Fruitfulness Through Abiding: Commit to daily practices that keep you connected to Christ, such as prayer, meditation, and reading Scripture. Recognize that your abundantly fruitful life is a direct result of your abiding in Him.

Intimately Intentional Living: Make conscious decisions that align with your identity in Christ. Set intentions for how you can live out your faith in your actions, words, and choices every day.

Now Remain In: Hold fast to your connection with Jesus throughout the day. In moments of uncertainty, remind yourself of His love and promises, and choose to remain in Him.

Engage in Joyful Obedience: Approach God's commands with a heart of joy. Look for ways to express your love for Him through obedience, finding delight in His ways.

As you walk through life, let these principles of R.E.F.I.N.E. guide you into a deeper relationship with Christ. By recognizing the true vine, embracing pruning, abiding for fruitfulness, living with intention, remaining steadfast, and obeying with joy, you will not only navigate the complexities of life but thrive within them, exhibiting the love and joy that comes from a life truly lived in Jesus.

To be refined is to be transformed by God's hand—shaped, purified, and prepared for His purpose. It's a process of turning rough, unpolished potential to a gleaming manifestation of divine intention. Refinement, though challenging, leads to a more profound understanding and closer relationship with God. Without refinement, one remains stagnant; with it, there is a blossoming of character, wisdom, and spiritual depth where we see God at work in our lives. The benefits of embracing this process are immense: a life that is rich with purpose, grounded in love, and abundantly fruitful. Follow the R.E.F.I.N.E. path, and turn your life towards a life unending JOY—a steadfast and internal joy, despite any external circumstances.

The Vine

It's no coincidence how you created the vine

Intentionally crafted by design

The blood of life flows through the veins

Abide in one another, you shall remain

A silhouette heart in every leaf

Love one another, we believe

Kneel before you with prayers expectant

In Your peace and strength, I am resilient

Pressed into seeking produces fruitfulness

Forever faithful in Your holiness

Much dreaded process, to refine

Promises abundant life, abiding in the vine

ABOUT THE AUTHOR

Lori McAfee is a story coach, speaker, author, and podcast host of *Get Your Rear in Gear*. With an unwavering faith in Jesus, Lori is devoted to making a positive difference in people's lives with her encouraging words of wisdom and uplifting spirit. In 2023, she wrote her first book, *Burning Hope*, a modern take on Christian romance in a Southern town, based on a true story. Lori lives in Calhoun, Georgia with her family. *The Refinery* is her second book.

Made in the USA
Columbia, SC
09 July 2024

38141888R00046